THE ONLY BOOK OF ITS KIND
REVEALING THE TRUE LANGUAGE
OF ITALY: THE HAND GESTURE!

FUNNY AND ORIGINAL, THIS
GUIDE WILL BE A FUN PURCHASE
READERS WILL WANT TO GET
FOR THEMSELVES AS WELL
AS FRIENDS AND RELATIVES.

LANGUAGE STUDENTS AND
TRAVELERS WILL FIND IT AN
INVALUABLE LESSON IN
REAL LIFE ITALIAN!

ITALIAN
WITHOUT WORDS:
An Illustrated Guide
to Italian Hand Gestures

ITALIAN WITHOUT WORDS:

An Illustrated Guide to Italian Hand Gestures

Written and Illustrated by

Jay Leone

S.p.i.
BOOKS

A division of Shapolsky Publishers, Inc.

S.P.I. BOOKS

A division of Shapolsky Publishers, Inc.

Copyright © 1992 by Jay Leone

For any additional information, contact:
S.P.I. BOOKS/Shapolsky Publishers, Inc.
136 West 22nd Street
New York, NY 10011
(212) 633-2022
FAX (212) 633-2123

ISBN: 1-56171-026-1

10 9 8 7 6 5 4 3 2 1

Printed and bound in the United States of America

To the pasta lovers . . .

... of the world

Italian
Without Words:
The First And Only Guide To Italy's Second Language

TABLE OF CONTENTS

THE HISTORY OF
HAND GESTURES

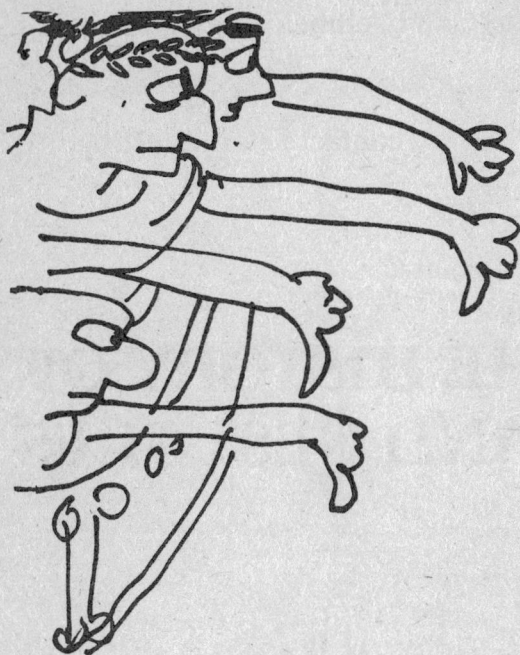

The art of hand gestures has a long and honorable history, dating back to the time of the Romans, the Egyptians of the Pharaohs and the early American Indians.

As civilization progressed the use of the hand motion to embellish or supplement speech diminished. A pity, as this has made human contact less interesting.

I remember as a youngster often being admonished to "Stop talking with your hands". Despite this, the Italians resisted this trend as gesticulating is almost second nature to them. The pressure to assimilate has caused this custom to wane somewhat but it still

is an important part of the everyday
speech of the Italians. In Italy I found
it enchantingly prevalent still. I marveled
at their use of gestures and was intrigued
by the richness it gave to their daily
communication.

So ingrained is this reliance on a

gesture to complete a verbal expression
that a true practitioner is left speechless
if forced to fall back on words alone. In
the neighborhood I grew up in there was
a man named Nicole, an old paesano
who had immigrated to America and
retained an inordinate fondness for the

well chosen gesture. As a joke, and perhaps to prove a point, a group of rambunctious guys one day physically restrained Nicole's arms and defied him to continue his conversation. Not surprisingly, poor Nicole was left unable to utter a word!

It was as if he had been gagged.

SICILY

WHEN YOU
ARE IN . . . .

SICILY . . . .

A few years ago, I drove to a Sicilian village to see some very important Byzantine mosaics. The parking area I came upon seemed a bit isolated and I became uneasy about the security of my car. I approached a Sicilian nearby,

hoping he could reassure me, and asked
in my limited Italian: "La mia machina
e sicura qui?" (Is my car safe here?).
Without saying a word he replied—
and his hand gestures delivered the
message perfectly!

HERE

The downward thrust of the pointed finger in a repetitive motion.

STEALING

A roll of the fingers (an almost universal symbol for stealing).

ISN'T TOLERATED

The raised forefinger swinging back and forth like the pendulum of a clock.

He couldn't have been more explicit!

NAPLES

WHEN YOU
ARE IN . . . .

NAPLES . . . .

While planning a trip to that beautiful city by the sea, Naples, friends in Rome warned me that although the Neopolitans are a warm and friendly people, there is an element, as in most tourist centers, that regards all tourists as fair game.

Briefed on some defensive measures I proceeded to that fair city. Upon arrival, I engaged a taxi and gave the driver the address of my pensione. Although my accent left much to be desired, I managed to make the brief instructions sound convincingly native Italian.

I avoided any conversation that might give me away as straniero (foreigner) and arrived at the destination. I braced myself when 'Il conto' (the fare) was about to be announced. As had been predicted, I was being conned.

The price quoted by the driver was indeed exorbitant. I immediately set into motion the hand gesture which my Roman friends had instructed me to use. It worked beautifully. Without even a word, the price came down to what it should have been. Here's what ensued . . . .

Stare your opponent straight in the eyes. Hold forefinger and thumb together and tap your forehead repeatedly like a hammer in a bell. Repeat until the price comes down to your satisfaction.

This is another gesture with somewhat the same meaning, except that it refers to a person nearby whose mental condition is dubious. It is a universal gesture.

While rotating the forefinger of one
hand, point the thumb of the other hand
in the direction of the person in question.

ROME

WHEN YOU
ARE IN . . . .

ROME . . . .

It is in Rome that one sees the most significant display of hand gestures. The policemen conducting traffic from the podium of the main intersection is the equal of the leader of a hundred-piece orchestra . . . . . . pure Toscanini!!

A slight twirl of the wrist gives more meaning to the flow of traffic than all the whistle blowing of a New York City traffic cop.

. . . and it is also in Rome that you will encounter the most chaotic traffic of any big city. The sweet nature of the Italians seems to vanish as they get behind their four-wheeled chargers. Be prepared to be on the receiving end of this gesture if you fail to respond at the wheel as the Italians think you should.

Middle finger raised, no motion involved. A steady display gets the message across. If you intend to use this gesture flee from the scene quickly.

There are other forms of 'Up yours', with subtle differences that vary from region to region in Italy. However, the differences are mostly in form. This gesture is more slowly and dramatic when a broader stage is available.

With arm extended, the flat of the
hand of the opposite arm comes down
on it at the elbow.

The hangout in Rome for the creative people, including the movie crowd, was Rosanti's Cafe, where one could see Moravia, DeChirico, Mastroianni and other notables enjoying aperitifs or espressos. As the eating hour approaches a meaningful signal is given . . . . . . mangiamo! (Let's eat!)

With the flat of the hand held palm down, the side of the body is struck in a chopping motion.

APPRECIATION

EXPRESSING
YOUR
APPRECIATION....

THE ITALIAN
WAY......

There is no place in the world where beauty is held in higher esteem that in Italy. When an Italian catches sight of an attractive woman he might stop in his tracks to express his admiration with this gesture. (She should not be insulted but rather regard this as a compliment.)

**Forefinger to the cheek, pressing
inward and rolling back and forth.**

This macho gesture, quite lascivious,
is another way of expressing not only
admiration but sexual desire. This is
a street corner display of 'Gallismo' –
Italian for machismo; it is low brow
and done surreptitiously.

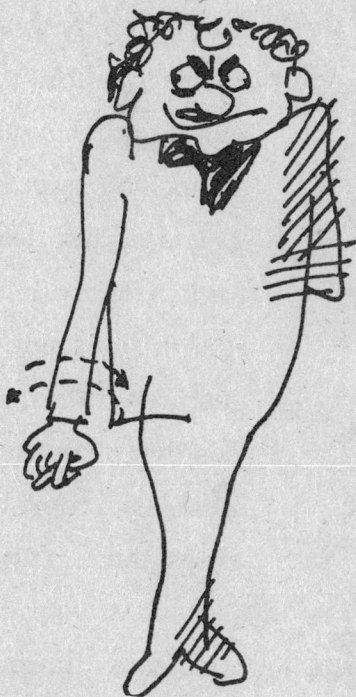

Arm thrust downward, clenched fist, thumb between fingers, and arm rolled back and forth.

Another suggestive gesture is often used by the young machos of **R**ome when a young signorina passes by. **I**t is used to provoke, for it is highly doubtful that this obscene gesture will bring a positive response. **B**ut, as in most big cities, there is always group of young men who enjoy flaunting their new found masculinity.

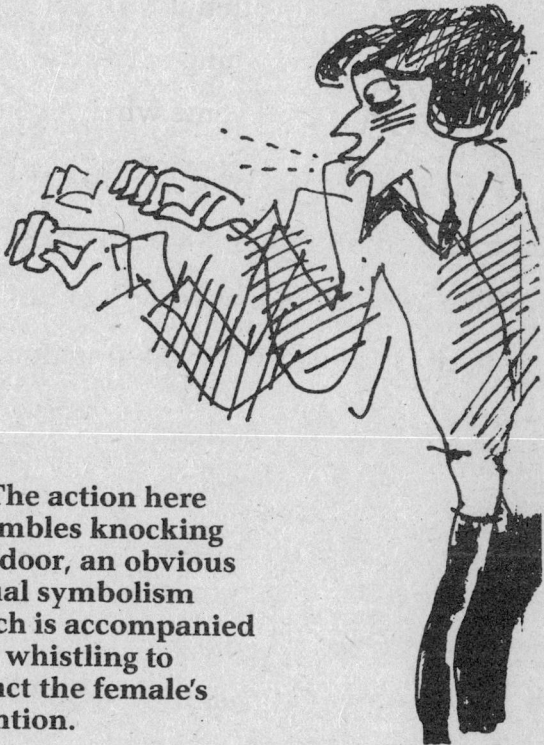

The action here
resembles knocking
at a door, an obvious
sexual symbolism
which is accompanied
by a whistling to
attract the female's
attention.

This non-verbal "Wow" is also used to express admiration for a beauty going by. The loose, limp hand gesture also emphasizes the enormity of a situation.

The hand, held up to shoulder height,
is swung vigorously in a pendulum-like
action.

Another acknowledgment of excellence of performance, service, beauty. Certainly no words are needed here.

The forefinger and thumb to the mouth as though being kissed and then tossed outward.

Bravo! Terrific! Great! . . . . all these
sentiments can best be expressed without
uttering a word. It would not be amiss,
in a ristorante or travola calda, to show
appreciation in this manner.

**Illustration is self-explanatory.
It indicates excellence.**

Sometimes, on a crowded bus or on a tram during rush hour a macho character gets carried away by the proximity of beauty. Taking advantage of the crowded situation he may use his loose hand to pinch the gluteous maximis of the female. Interestingly enough, it seems always to be the tourists who report these incidents.

This is always performed with a look of total innocence.

A pat on the tummy expresses gastronomical approval. Even if your limited Italian can't express satisfaction, this will certainly please the cameriere (waiter) and sometimes be just as welcome as a tip.

HELLOS, GOODBYES

SAYING HELLO
OR GOODBYE . . . .

THE ITALIAN
WAY.....

Greetings and partings are very emotional affairs among Italians. It would be quite normal for your host to greet you with a strong embrace and kissing on both cheeks, regardless of gender.

The bear hug is usually followed by a kiss on the right cheek and then on the left. Don't be surprised if a kiss is even planted on the lips.

This pleasant expression of goodbye may be recalled by movie buffs from the early De Sica movies. Sometimes it is accompanied by a jaunty, 'Ciao', but it is equally alone.

Cup the hands toward you and execute the movement back and forth a few times . . . . or for an indefinite period of time.

'Let's split' is a nice gesture to indicate departure without saying a word. At Rosati's cafe or a cocktail party, you can use this to signal your partner from across the crowded room.

The flat of the hand is used in a chopping motion with the palm of the opposite hand while moving both hands away from your body.

In Rome you see women summoning someone with an arm motion that better suggests pushing away. This is an oddity that I have noted in most Latin countries.

One hand, with the palm facing
outward, is pushed away repeatedly.

Another form of beckoning has a conspiratorial quality about it, as if to say, "I have a proposition you can't afford to refuse".

The hooked forefinger motions toward
you while simultaneously the arm is
moved away from you.

AGGRESSIONS

TAKING
OUT YOUR
AGGRESSIONS....

THE ITALIAN
WAY.....

It is typical of some Italians, as well
as other Mediterranean people, to display
a lack of patience in queuing up in line.
I have waged total war against seemingly
old ladies who push ahead of me in line.
A very well dressed woman once tried to
squeeze ahead of me at Rinascente, a
popular department store in Rome.
Without even 'Tocca a me' (I'm next),
I slammed my fist on the counter and
was immediately waited on.

A strong hard-fisted slam on the counter will ensure attention and your rightful place in line.

This is 'Cornuto', a gesture usually directed at someone with whom an Italian male has had an altercation. When offended he will use this in an aggressive way, accusing his opponent of being a cuckold. This is indeed the strongest insult one can deliver to a man in Italy.

Eyes fixed on your opponent, fire away with the horn gesture. The forefinger and little finger are the horns.

Beware the person giving this non-verbal expression. The thumb treatment is a curse wishing great harm to the person against whom it is directed. This is a very Southern Italian gesture, especially common in Sicily.

Put the thumb to your teeth, almost in a bite, and throw it forward. Very potent stuff.

This is a very ominous gesture, connoting the situation is hopeless. It can also refer to someone who has wronged you: 'He's going to get it'. It's a very universal and explicit sign.

The action here suggests cutting off the head – signifying the finality of the situation.

SUPERSTITIONS

SUPERSTITIOUS
IN NATURE . . .

THE ITALIAN
WAY.....

A lot of gestures fall into the realm of superstition. Often the sign of the cross is called into play to avert bad luck. The Church, no doubt takes a dim view of this. I recall seeing my mother, during a thunder storm, put her fingers to her forehead and perform this ritual, or an ambulance going by, might also necessitate making the sign of the cross. Even those men who take their religion with a dose of skepticism surreptitiously mark the cross on their foreheads—just to be on the safe side.

A surreptitious crossing of the
fingers is believed to ward off bad luck.
Sometimes, if a white lie is being told,
this is put to use so as not to be punished
by celestial authorities. Children will
often use this gesture to guard against
corporal reprimands when telling a lie.

Done unobtrusively with the right hand.

An Italian prizefighter would not think of commencing a fight without the proper safeguard of making the sign of the cross. It is both a silent prayer and an assurance that bad luck will be kept away.

Just before the gong the boxer goes back to his corner and performs this brief ritual. That this is no assurance against being knocked out, Primo Carnera discovered many years ago in his bout with Max Baer.

A funeral passing
by is a serious affair. An
Italian who happens
upon one takes certain
measures to ward off
any adverse luck that
might result from his
encounter. Holding the
genitals (and not always
surreptitiously) is an
assurance of one's con-
tinued virility. Well
dressed, seemingly middle class
gentlemen have been seen holding their
crotch when a hearse passes by.

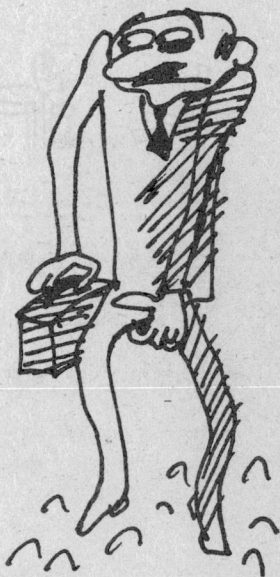

The arms crossed is a begging for pity or sympathy. It is after a tale has been told. A way of saying, 'Believe me it is true.' It is also used spontaneously as an expression of surprise; my mother used to get a lot of mileage out of this one.

Italian women seem to use this expression most frequently. It is generally followed with a 'Dio Mio'. Used quite often in the course of every day life.

This prayer-like gesture when used to appeal to someone, begs for understanding in a hopeless situation. I used this gesture, for example, when the repairs on my car weren't finished when promised.

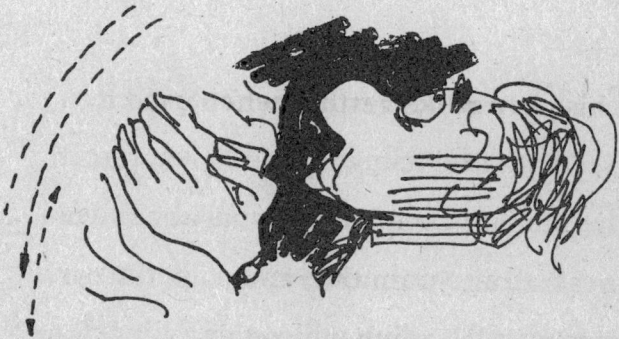

Executed just like praying, but the
hands are moved up and down to make
the pleading more emphatic.

When my car still wasn't repaired, a friend advised using tears as a last resort. The Italians seem very casual about deadlines and appointments and sometimes no amount of pleading will get anything done on time. But they can respond with alacrity to a lachrimonious display of emotion. The tears worked.

No hands or words are needed, just a simple stare and an exaggerated look of remorse. Tears, if you produce them, gets results.

CHARACTER

CHARACTER
ANALYSES....

THE ITALIAN
WAY.....

He's gay. Signor Domenicucci, a
tailor, when asked about a friend that I
had recommended, made this implicit
sign. The Italians, however, show a great
tolerance toward gays.

The ear lobe is held with the forefinger
and thumb of either right or left hand
and the head is slightly tilted in the
direction of the person in question.

This gesture signifies that a person is shrewd, wise or sharp. A few years ago at Porta Portese, the flea market in Rome, a proprietor of one of the stalls used this when a friend, seemingly, got the best of bargain. (A rather rare feat considering that the dealers usually outsmart the customers there.)

The pinky of one hand pushes down
the lower eyelid, while the thumb of the
other hand points to the shrewd one. This
is a high compliment.

This gesture is used mostly as a warning or to advise caution; watch the kettle and see that it doesn't boil over, is the way the Italians would put it. Be alert! Be on guard!

The forefinger of the right hand rubbing the side of the nose up and down in a very knowing way.

ATTITUDES

A REFLECTION
ON ATTITUDES....

THE ITALIAN
WAY......

A negative reply can be executed with a simple flip of the head. It is a very Mediterranean gesture, perhaps imported by the Saracens. The Arabs accompany it with a cluck of the tongue, as do some Italians.

A fixed stare and a quick flip of the head will get the message across when 'No' is the answer.

How are
things?
What's new?
You can
reply in
either of
two ways.
When the
finger is
pointed and
given a
circular
movement,

**The pointed finger
might be an indication
of a deal being so-so.**

the response means that a deal or
commercial venture is only so-so. When
the flat of the hand is given a rotating
movement, it might mean the situation in
general is **OK.**

The flat of the hand in a rotating gesture says all is OK.

This is a questioning gesture. What's up? What's going on? What are you talking about? It means all these things. When coming on a scene of which he disapproved, my father would respond with this gesture.

The forefinger and thumb touch as the hand moves up and down. You, meanwhile, grimace disapprovingly of course.

When old cronies and paesani come to visit, my father would simply make this gesture, sometimes with a wink. Without so much as a word, he was clearly understood and the bottle was brought out. The imbibing would commence.

**The thumb is directed to the mouth
and a slightly lifted pinky suggests, if the
occasion warrants, mock politeness.**

MISCELLANEOUS....

This is a kind of 'Devil may care' expression: What do I care or 'Che me ne frega' as the Italians would say. It's a gesture that I recall my father performing when mom reprimanded him for not amounting to anything.

The back of the hand is put under the chin and thrust forward, palm up. Just once is enough to get the message across.

Unlike the supplicating hand gesture this has many meanings pertaining to the body, all sexual in significance. The one illustrated here makes references to a woman's sexual activities. It is very 'X' rated and generally a street corner expression.

The thumb, forefinger and middle finger are touching and the hand movement is up and down. The expression on the face is lascivious, naturally.

During a conversation in Rome an Italian friend stopped abruptly to describe a situation that was short of perfection. With his hand, he simulated a 'T' in mid-air, perfect to the 'T'.

If walking, come to a immediate halt. The stance must be erect, the body at military attention and the gesture executed perfectly.

Upon catching me in a compromising situation with the neighbor's daughter, my aunt responded with this gesture. It's a sign of moral criticism or condemnation and admonishment. Used often with children, accompanied with 'Peesh bee shame', this is typically Italo-American but not unknown in other ethnic communities.

A stern glance is followed by crossing the fingers, a slicing motion done repeatedly.

This is an expression of futility as if to say, "What's the use?" It suggests that fate is beyond one's control and is accompanied sometimes with a simple 'Beh' (You may not find that word in the dictionary, but a loose translation would be 'so what').

An entire body movement is required.
Stand off a few paces and execute in a
lazy fashion: shoulders raised, hands
beseeching with palms up.

What has been shown in this little book is but a fraction of the hand gestures commonly used in Italy and the Italo-American communities of the United States. Like much in the vernacular, regional variations should be expected.

You can not, of course, travel through Italy using nothing but your hands to communicate. But you will certainly ingratiate yourself with the Italians by supplementing your language skills with the easily understood and appreciated hand gestures.